DON'T START WITHOUT ME

A Comedy

by

JOYCE RAYBURN

SAMUEL FRENCH

LONDON
NEW YORK TORONTO SYDNEY HOLLYWOOD

© 1972 BY JOYCE RAYBURN

ISBN 0 573 01112 5

MADE AND PRINTED IN GREAT BRITAIN BY
LATIMER TREND AND CO. LTD, PLYMOUTH

MADE IN ENGLAND

DON'T START WITHOUT ME

First presented by Bill Freedman and Charles Kasher at the Harrogate Theatre on 7th November 1970, later transferring to the Garrick Theatre on 10th February 1971 with the following cast of characters:

Eric	Paul Daneman
Vivien	Jan Waters
Norman	Brian Cox
Ruth	Lucy Fleming

The play produced by Barry Morse
Setting by Alan Green

The action passes in a house in North London

ACT I

    Scene 1   An evening in July
    Scene 2   The following Saturday afternoon

ACT II

    Scene 1   Late the same evening
    Scene 2   The following morning

Time - the present

ACT 1

SCENE 1

A house in North London. Just after six o'clock on an evening in July. It is raining

As the CURTAIN *rises, Vivien enters the hall, loaded with shopping and carrying a dripping umbrella. She shuts the front door with her foot, puts the umbrella in the stand, unlocks the door to Eric's flat and enters, again shutting the door with her foot. She then proceeds to dash about the flat, changing into casual wear and Scholl sandals while simultaneously unpacking the shopping, putting something on the stove to cook, clearing away remnants of the morning's breakfast, shoving some flowers into a vase, etc. Eventually she exits to the bedroom*

In complete contrast, Eric enters slowly, lets himself into the flat, allows his mac to drop from the chair to the floor, dumps his briefcase

The bedroom door opens

Vivien (*off*) Is that you, Eric?
Eric Of course it's me. Who else has got the key to this flat?
Vivien (*off*) Nobody.
Eric I'm glad to hear it.
Vivien (*off*) Who else would have a key to the flat?
Eric I've no idea.
Vivien (*off*) So why suggest that somebody has?
Eric Oh, my God. I came in and you called out, "Is that you, Eric?"

Vivien enters

Vivien It was meant as a form of greeting.
Eric Really. Well, "Good evening" is a form of greeting. "Hallo" is a form of greeting. And "Hallo, darling," would make a pleasant change.
Vivien Hallo. Darling. And how long is darling going to leave darling's sopping wet coat lying on the floor?
Eric (*pouring himself a sherry*) Just as long as darling feels so inclined.
Vivien It'll look like a chewed rag in the morning.
Eric So shall I, probably.
Vivien (*shaking Eric's coat*) Filthy weather.
Eric Yes—very nasty.
Vivien Don't pour one for me, whatever you do.
Eric Sorry. What would you like?
Vivien Nothing, thanks. I thought you might have offered that's all.

Eric I'm offering now.

Vivien I've no time.

Eric What are you doing, for heaven's sake?

Vivien Everything—as always.

Eric Here it comes. The evening's martyrdom.

Vivien We've got to eat, haven't we?

Eric I suppose so. Eventually.

Vivien Eventually's your favourite word. You should have it for an epitaph. Here lies Eric Elliott, who died of sheer inertia—eventually.

Eric Don't be so bloody morbid. The best hour of the day. The first healing drink, and you turn it sour.

Vivien Oh, go ahead. Enjoy your healing drink. That's your evening's exercise. Lifting your elbow.

Eric I get all the exercise I want trying to keep out of your slipstream. Can't you relax for one moment?

Vivien I seem to have lost the knack.

Eric If you ever had it. Why can't you be like me?

Vivien Relaxed?

Eric Exactly.

Vivien Bone idle.

Eric There's no need to exaggerate, sweetheart.

Vivien I couldn't.

Eric You're murder to live with lately.

Vivien Am I?

Eric For some reason, the mere sight of me—at peace with myself and the world about me—drives you into a frenzy.

Vivien Perhaps I should have a drink after all.

Eric Good idea. You're not so exhausting when you're sloshed. (*He gives her a sherry*)

Norman enters the hall with two suitcases

Vivien Listen. I think they're back.

Eric Who? The lodgers?

Vivien Don't call them that. Norman owns his half of the house.

Eric The top half. So it feels like having lodgers.

Vivien He didn't want the ground floor.

Eric I'm not surprised. With you galloping about over his head.

Vivien You were both installed long before I came.

Norman goes out

It's more likely that he didn't want to hear you and your birds galloping about overhead.

Eric Birds? What birds? Before you brought your sleeping bag, this place was a monastery.

Vivien Some monastery!

Eric Except for week-ends and public holidays.

Norman brings on two more cases, with a wet raincoat over his head, then goes out again

I thought they were due home tomorrow?

Vivien No, today. (*She opens the flat door*)

Eric I wish you'd decide whether you're going in or out. You're making a draught.

Vivien I don't want it to look as though I'm spying on them.

Eric Shut the door, then.

Vivien shuts the flat door

Norman carries Ruth in and puts her down in the hall

Vivien Ought we to greet them in the hall or wait until they call on us?

Eric Do what you like.

Vivien What d'you think?

Eric I think you're making an enormous issue out of it.

Vivien After all, they are coming back from their honeymoon. I wouldn't want to embarrass them.

Eric I would.

Vivien Listen, you're not to make any of your funny remarks.

Eric Like for instance?

Vivien Like, for instance, "how was the weather—or didn't you notice?"

Eric I promise not to mention the weather.

Norman takes the cases upstairs

Vivien It's hard to know what to say. "Did you have a good honeymoon?" doesn't sound right.

Eric "Did you have a good time?" sounds worse.

Vivien Honeymoon's such a silly word.

Eric Almost as silly as going out to Tenerife to do what you can do at home.

Vivien Ruth chose Tenerife.

Eric Ah, Ruth. Such a nice girl! I hope he remembered to take his flannel pyjamas.

Norman comes back for Ruth and carries her upstairs

Vivien She may be quite warm-hearted—underneath.

Eric She may indeed. On the other hand, if you see the tip of an iceberg, you don't bank on finding hot chocolate sauce below.

Vivien You never know. We only met her a few times.

Eric Yes. Norman was always down at Guildford with her people. Home movies and digestive biscuits. Beats me why he kept going back.

Vivien He loved her.

Eric He wanted her.

Vivien Same thing.

Eric Not necessarily. If he goes on wanting her after he's had her, that could be love.

Vivien I'm sure he will.

Eric It's a gamble, though, isn't it. Better to find out in advance.

Vivien Perhaps he did.

Eric Want to bet?

Vivien You can't tell by looking at the girl.

Eric I can tell by looking at Norman. And when he did bring her here, you could have set your watch by the time she left. Ten o'clock. On the dot.

Vivien She had to get back to Guildford.

Eric Why?

Vivien Because she's a bright girl, and I wish I'd done that.

Eric But you don't know anyone in Guildford.

Vivien I mean I should have held out on you.

Eric You couldn't have. You're not that sort.

Vivien I'm a fool in other words.

Eric Since when is it foolish to have a warm, generous nature.

Vivien Since I let you take advantage of it.

Eric You've never talked like that before.

Vivien No. I'm starting now. We've been living together for two years, and . . .

Eric As long as that?

Vivien Longer if you count that month in Leicester.

Eric Yes. A trial run in the provinces before coming to Town. Rave notices and over three hundred performances.

Vivien Well over that, if you include matinees.

Eric Have you been keeping a log?

Vivien And I've been thinking.

Eric You're not paid to think.

Vivien I'm not paid at all.

Eric A girl of independent means.

Vivien I have a job.

Eric That's the spirit.

Vivien Anyway, since we went to Norman's wedding—

Eric This sounds ominous . . .

Vivien —I've come to the conclusion that there's a lot to be said in favour of good old-fashioned matrimony.

Eric True. There is a lot to be said. Most of it sentimental bull.

Vivien We always said we'd get married one day.

Eric Well, yes, eventually.

Vivien I reckon it's eventually now.

Eric Is this why you've been bashing the pan-lids about?

Vivien I suppose so. It's been on my mind.

Eric I'm glad you told me. I thought you were going off your rocker.

Vivien I wasn't sure how you'd take it.

Eric I take it as I take everything. A wise man bows to the inevitable.

Vivien You mean you don't mind.

Eric Of course not. It's perfectly natural that you should feel this way.

Vivien Darling! We can invite Ruth and Norman and take them for a meal afterwards.

Eric Not tonight, sweetheart. They won't feel like turning out tonight.

Vivien Well, of course, it couldn't be tonight.

Eric Next week, some time.

Vivien Saturday's best. It takes a few days to get a licence in any case.

Eric A licence?

Vivien You've got to have a licence.

Eric To go out to dinner?

Vivien No. To get married.

Eric Who's getting married?

Vivien We are.

Eric You may be. But I'm not. Top me up, there's a good girl. (*He holds out his glass*)

Vivien But you agreed. (*She refills Eric's glass and gives it to him*)

Eric When?

Vivien Just now.

Eric When? When? Mind what you're doing.

Ruth comes downstairs

Vivien You said it was perfectly natural.

Eric Perfectly natural for you to feel that way is what I meant. Get a cloth.

Vivien But you said you didn't mind.

Eric Which shows what a tolerant chap I am. Get a cloth.

Ruth knocks at the flat door

God, I'm ankle deep in Harvey's.

Vivien I hope you drown in it.

Vivien exits to the bedroom

Eric (*calling after her*) Damn it all, Viv. I allow you your prejudices, the least you can do is allow me mine.

Ruth knocks again

Vivien. Be reasonable. Oh, hell! (*He opens the door*) What d'you want? Oh, sorry. I thought it was Norman.

Ruth No, it's me. Hallo.

Eric Hallo, Ruth. Come in.

Ruth Well—just for a moment. (*She enters the flat*)

Eric I'm trying to get rid of this sherry. I can't stand to see half-empty bottles hanging around.

Ruth That one's half-full.

Eric It depends on your point of view. Never mind. Good for the carpet.

Ruth Is it?

Eric Oh, yes. Mother always cleaned the rugs with Amontillado. (*He gets rid of the bottle and glass*) You're looking well.

Ruth I feel well.

Eric In fact you look great.

Ruth Thank you.

Eric It must be the tan. It suits you. Are you that colour all over?

Ruth Well—not quite.

Eric No, of course not. Am I staring?

Ruth Just a bit.

Eric You look so different. Last time I saw you, you were trailing clouds of white lace.

Ruth There were five yards in the skirt alone.

Eric Is that so? You were looking fairly white yourself.

Ruth I was nervous.

Eric All pinched and wan and virg . . . verging on the anaemic almost. How's Norman?

Ruth A lot better, thanks. Getting over the worst.

Eric Oh?

Ruth Will your wife be very long?

Eric My wife?

Ruth I wonder if she remembered to take some milk for us?

Eric Milk—ah—that's not my department.

Ruth Perhaps you could ask her.

Eric Yes. All right.

Ruth Am I being an awful nuisance?

Eric Not at all. Vivien.

Eric opens the bedroom door and a slipper flies out

Oh, good. I was looking for that. Thank you, darling. (*He puts it on*) That's better.

Ruth Where's the other one?

Eric No doubt it will turn up—eventually.

Ruth I'll call back, shall I?

Eric What for?

Ruth For the milk.

Eric Oh, that. Oh, yes. (*He approaches the bedroom door, changes his mind and returns*) There'll be some in the fridge. She'll have popped it in the fridge. Yes, that's where it'll be. In the fridge.

Ruth Oh. (*She goes to get it, then pops back*) There's something boiling over. Shall I switch it off?

Norman comes downstairs

Eric Not my department.

Ruth I think I'd better.

Ruth exits to the kitchen

Eric (*going to the bedroom door*) Vivien. Darling, open the door.

Norman enters the flat

Norman Want any help?

Eric Don't creep up on me like that.

Norman Sorry. The door was open.

Eric I'll make sure it doesn't happen again.

Ruth (*looking in from the kitchen*) Norman? I'm just wiping this stove down. There's tomato soup all over the hot-plates.

Eric She looks marvellous. I wish I could say the same for you.

Norman Thanks.

Eric Well, why is your face the colour of mouldy hay? People are supposed to look better after a holiday, not worse.

Norman Holiday? You've got to be joking. (*Extending a shaking hand*) Look at that.

Eric Who are you waving to?

Norman Look here. See that.

Eric You are in a bad way.

Norman I'm lucky to be alive. If I'd known what I was in for!

Eric Didn't you?

Norman I'd read about it.

Eric Well, you can't tell by reading about it.

Norman They make it sound so attractive.

Eric It can be fun.

Norman All those colour pictures. Very deceptive.

Eric What book's this?

Norman We got dozens of them.

Eric Did you?

Norman They caught me once, but never again—you can count me out from now on!

Eric Never?

Norman Never. I've told Ruth.

Eric Doesn't she object?

Norman Why should she? She's my wife, isn't she?

Eric I would have thought that was the whole point.

Norman She doesn't want to kill me.

Eric No, but . . .

Norman Not my fault my mother had red hair.

Eric Norman—you really ought to go and see a doctor.

Norman I'm going to. First thing in the morning.

Eric Ruth's fairly bouncing with health.

Norman It was fine for her. She enjoyed every minute of it.

Ruth enters

Ruth I couldn't leave it. It bakes on hard. (*She looks at Norman and then at Eric*) Has he been complaining?

Eric He let the odd word slip.

Ruth The trouble was it was too hot for him.

Eric So I gather.

Ruth He's got this fair skin, from his mother's side of the family.

Norman I came down with heatstroke.

Eric What? Oh, I see.

Norman What?

Eric Nothing.

Ruth And then something bit him.

Norman A tarantula.

Ruth They didn't think it was a tarantula, darling.

Norman They lied in their teeth. They were only interested in hushing it up. Why don't they put that in their brochures? Come to Tenerife and be bitten by man-eating spiders.

Ruth You didn't actually see it.

Norman I saw the marks of its fangs.

Ruth How could you?

Norman By improvising a rough periscope.

Ruth He was lying on his face for a week.

Eric What a shame!

Norman Cooped up in a darkened room, while Ruth was down by the swimming pool—having a whale of a time.

Ruth You wanted me to go out.

Norman Yes, I know. I hope I'm not selfish.

Ruth Could you look at a glass of warm milk now, darling?

Norman Must I?

Ruth Well, you lost your lunch on the plane. You've got to have something. You need building up.

Ruth exits upstairs

Norman Have you got any brandy?

Eric Help yourself.

Norman Still the same old Eric. Wouldn't give a dying man a drink of water.

Eric You didn't ask for water.

Norman I meant, do I have to get up for it?

Eric I'm sorry. No, of course you don't have to get up for it. In your condition. You stay right where you are.

Norman Thanks.

Eric And do without.

Norman I should know you by now.

Eric If I did everything people expected of me, I'd be an old man by the time I was eighty.

Norman How's the little woman?

Eric Playing me up for some reason. And incidentally, why does Ruth refer to her as my wife?

Norman Probably because she's under that impression.

Eric Haven't you told her?

Norman The subject never arose, and I thought the less said, the better.

Eric To listen to you one would think you were living over a brothel. There are other ties just as binding as legal ones.

Norman Try explaining that to my in-laws.

Eric You can tell Ruth to keep it to herself.

Norman She tells Mummy everything.

Eric That's your problem. What did you have to go and get married for, anyway?

Norman You know damn well what for.

Eric It doesn't seem to have done you much good.

Norman I shall be a new man now I'm in my natural element, and I don't expect to be jeered at.

Eric You won't get any sympathy from me after the trouble you've caused with your confetti and rice.

Norman Why, what's wrong?

Eric D'you know what Vivien's doing in there?

Norman Changing?

Eric You've hit it. Changing. Changing from a sweet loving girl into a Victorian maiden. Suddenly, after two years of unwedded bliss, it's a fate worse than death. The thought wouldn't have entered her head, if you hadn't set the clock back a hundred years with your grey topper and pink carnation.

Norman Oh, I see. She wants the plain gold ring.

Eric Shush. Not so loud. With any luck, she may forget all about it.

Norman You've been pushing your luck for too long.

Eric It's not all one way, you know. The benefit's mutual.

Norman Women never think so.

Eric They can be re-educated, and kept away from contaminating influences. I would never have taken you in, if I'd known you were going to get mixed up with a respectable girl.

Norman You took me in because you couldn't afford to buy this place on your own.

Eric I did it to save you from a rat-infested cellar.

Norman A very nice basement flat.

Eric And a landlord whose leanings were suspect.

Norman Well, how was I to know. Just because he offered to knit me a scarf.

Eric You were in moral danger there, and too naïve to spot it, but if I'd suspected that you'd go racing off to the altar . . .

Norman It was the only way.

Eric You couldn't have tried hard enough.

Norman I didn't try at all. Ruth's not that sort of girl.

Eric Norman, dear Norman, there's only one sort of girl. It's the way they're handled that counts. Even living with one has its disadvantages. Women are a fidgety lot. But what's the alternative?

Norman Do without.

Eric Do without? That's sheer defeatism. No, the only alternative is to play the field. And that can be heavy going too.

Norman You used to cover a lot of ground.

Eric Yes, but when I remember the effort. The wear and tear on my nervous system. Nowadays I can skip the show and the supper and get on to the essentials. That's how it should be. On tap like hot water. I mean, suppose you had to start from scratch every time you wanted a bath. Rubbing two sticks together to make a fire.

Norman So you find the right girl and marry her.

Eric Correction. You find the right girl. Full stop.

Vivien dashes out of the bedroom and into the kitchen

She's been like that since I came home. Thanks to you.

Norman What have I got to do with it?

Vivien (*from the kitchen*) Who switched the soup off?

Eric Ruth did.

Vivien Oh. I didn't think it could have been you. Here's your other foot. Catch. (*She throws a slipper to Eric*)

Norman You ducked.

Eric I had my reasons.

Vivien (*coming down into the room*) Hallo, Norman.

Norman Hallo, love.

Vivien Have you had a good—was the weather—you're not very brown.

Eric He's been lying face down most of the time.

Vivien I told you not to say things like that.

Eric He said it first.

Norman I got my bottom bitten.

Vivien Oh, dear.

Eric By an insect.

Vivien Oh, an insect.

Eric You ought to be ashamed of yourself. Harbouring lewd thoughts.

Vivien And you didn't, I suppose?

Eric Darling, to the pure all things are pure.

Norman It turned septic.

Ruth comes downstairs

Eric Dear old Norman. Your name suits you. The norm. Plain and wholesome and I wish we'd never met.

Vivien What a thing to say! H'es just fed up because he knows it's time we followed your example.

Eric Hear that? Your example. My case rests.

Ruth enters the flat with the milk

Ruth Here we are. Hallo, there.

Vivien Hallo. Feeling warm?

Ruth It's muggy, isn't it?

Eric Let me take that.

Ruth Oh, thank you.

Eric I'll pop it down here. (*He puts the milk by the sofa*)

Norman See that. He moved!

Vivien Do be careful, darling. That arm of yours is going to be stiff tomorrow.

Eric No matter what I do, I'm in the wrong.

Ruth I gather you're not the sort of husband who helps with the chores.

Vivien What makes you think he's any sort of husband at all?

Eric Tell her, you great nit.

Ruth Tell who what?

Vivien Doesn't she know?

Ruth Don't I know what?

Eric Go on, Norman. It's your fault. If you hadn't been so bloody coy about it, you wouldn't have to make a public announcement.

Norman If you followed the rules, there wouldn't be one to make.

Eric I'm not going to arrange my private life to please your bloody in-laws. I'm jolly glad you got your arse bitten, I wish it had been a cobra.

Ruth I thought you two were friends.

Eric Not since he began to meddle in my affairs.

Norman I took me a wife. Is that meddling?

Eric And I didn't. So what?

Ruth You didn't? Aren't you? Aren't they . . . ?

Norman No, they're not.

Ruth Oh, oh well. It doesn't matter, does it? Nobody worries about that sort of thing any more.

Norman Daddy would.

Ruth Oh, blow Daddy. I'm not in Guilford now. I can do what I like.

Eric You'll have to watch her, Norman. She's got a wild gleam in her eye.

Ruth We haven't finished unpacking yet. Are you coming, darling?

Norman Yes, love.

Ruth You haven't touched your milk.

Norman I'm going to.

Eric opens the door

Ruth Bring it with you. (*To Eric*) Oh, thank you . . .

Ruth and Norman exit upstairs

Norman (*as he goes*) Be seeing you.

Vivien What's amusing you?

Eric Norman. He thinks he's the luckiest man in the world.

Vivien That's a nice way to feel.

Eric Did you notice how quickly even Ruth accepted the situation? That's the way it is now. Some do and some don't. You can choose.

Vivien It was simpler when there was no choice.

Eric But we're happy, aren't we?

Vivien How can you say that? You know how we fight.

Eric Married couples fight.

Vivien Not like us. We fight like two people who aren't sure of each other.

Eric I'm sure. I've always been sure. I'm a permanent fixture. Every bit as steady as old Norman. Just as normal. What more do you want?

Vivien Status.

Eric Status? You've never mentioned that before.

Vivien I never felt the lack of it so acutely before.

Eric Tell you what, sweetheart. We'll have supper by the telly and you can blow the froth off my beer.

Vivien No, I've made up my mind. It'll either be next week or never.

Eric Right. That suits me.

Vivien What suits you?

Eric What you suggest. Either next week or never. I'm absolutely with you there. We don't want it always hanging over our heads.

Vivien You're too subtle for me. I shall just have to leave you.

Eric Leave me?

Vivien That's what I'm trying to make you understand.

Eric I understood no such thing. You didn't say a word about leaving.

Vivien I'm sorry. But that's the position.

Eric I need time to think.

Vivien You've got a week from Saturday.

Eric A week? To decide on something which affects my whole future?

Vivien Our whole future.

Eric A week's nothing. I need at least a year.

Vivien You've had two years already.

Eric Ah, but listen, Vivien . . .

Vivien All right. If you hate the idea so much you can forget all about it.

Eric Can I really?

Vivien Don't give it another thought.

Eric Darling. I knew you'd see reason.

Vivien And I'll leave you.

Eric Hey, those are my tactics.

Vivien Where d'you suppose I learned them?

CURTAIN

SCENE 2

The same. The following Saturday afternoon

When the CURTAIN *rises Eric is alone, dressed in comfortable old clothes, lying on the sofa. The telephone rings, and he tries to answer it without getting up. Then it stops and he gets an orange from the kitchen and starts to peel it.*

Norman comes downstairs and knocks at the flat door

Norman Eric?

Eric Go to hell.

Norman Open the door.
Eric Was that you on the telephone just now?
Norman Yes. Why didn't you answer?
Eric I am incommunicado.
Norman You're behaving like a child.
Eric Good. Then I can't be married without my parents' consent.
Norman Let me in.
Eric No. Stop hammering on the door. You'll ruin the paintwork. Have you no respect for property.

Norman leaves and goes upstairs

Go away and leave me alone. I've only got seven days of freedom left—and then bang—another good man gone. (*He throws the peel into the waste-paper basket, often missing*) Sunday, Monday, Tuesday, etc. (*He goes into the hall*)

Norman enters from the bedroom

(*Returning to the flat*) How did you get in?
Norman I came down the fire-escape and through the window.
Eric You've got a bloody cheek. Which way are you going back? Through the kitchen and up the flue?
Norman Vivien asked me to look in on you.
Eric She didn't ask you to break in on me. How long are they going to take over their shopping?
Norman The message was to expect them when we see them.
Eric Charming. Vivien's got so many clothes already that my suits are huddled together at the end of the rail like penguins.
Norman She wanted something new. Something borrowed—something blue.
Eric Norman—I warn you. If you tie an old boot to my car I'll make you eat it.
Norman Have you had anything to eat?
Eric Not since breakfast.
Norman When was that?
Eric Half an hour ago.
Norman What time did you get up?
Eric Half an hour ago.
Norman I thought it was quiet down here.
Eric Have you had your ear pressed to the floor-boards?
Norman Listen, you can stay in bed indefinitely for all I care, but you won't solve anything that way.
Eric No, but I like to be miserable in comfort.
Norman Don't imagine your problems are going to disappear while you're curled up in a pre-natal position. They'll still be there when you get up, and the sooner you face them the better.

Eric Will you please take yourself and your homely wisdom off my territory.

Norman I'm only doing Vivien a favour.

Eric Do me one and get lost.

Norman Shall we watch the cricket?

Eric No, thanks.

Norman Or there's racing on the other side.

Eric I'm not in the mood.

Norman How about some music? (*Looking at the Radio Times*) Saturday. Saturday. Ah—*Afternoon Sequence. The Marriage of Figaro.*

Eric You've come to gloat, haven't you? You're glad to see me brought down to your level. All right, so I'm in a spot. But I'll find a way out.

Norman If you're like this now, what sort of state will you be in, in a week's time?

Eric Pretty desperate. But I won't go without a struggle. I'll resist to the end. There'll be a trail of blood leading to the Registrar's feet.

Norman Could you look at a cup of coffee?

Eric Good Lord. You're beginning to talk like Ruth. It's frightening. After a mere three weeks in captivity.

Norman You've got a warped view on marriage, Eric. I don't think you ought to go through with it.

Eric I've got no choice, have I?

Norman You can let Vivien go.

Eric No, I can't. I've got used to her. That's what happens. They move in and make themselves indispensable, and when you're thoroughly tamed and domesticated, they tie a little ribbon round your neck. Tight.

Norman You're devoted to her, aren't you?

Eric Besotted.

Norman So stop bellyaching and make her your wife.

Eric Ugh. Wife. The very sound of it puts me right off.

Norman I haven't noticed that the sight of my wife puts you off.

Eric Ah, now when it's someone else's, that's different.

Norman That's what's wrong with you. You've got a built-in inclination towards adultery. Unless a thing's illegal or immoral—preferably both —it doesn't appeal to you.

Eric If I want a potted analysis, I'll ask for it. Clear off. Go and analyse yourself and your built-in inclination to conform.

Norman (*moving towards the bedroom*) If everybody thought like you the whole fabric of society would crumble.

Eric It's rotten anyway.

Norman A child wouldn't know his father.

Eric That could be an advantage.

Norman A brother might marry his sister.

Eric Good luck to them.

Norman You've got to have some discipline. Some laws. You can't build a firm foundation on shifting sands.

Eric I'm not shifting. I'm constant. I'm static. I'm a rock.

Norman A rock doesn't object to being tied down.

Eric A rock doesn't need to be tied down. The whole exercise is super-
fluous, and it's the absurdity of it that I object to.
Norman Have you explained this to Vivien?
Eric I can't get through to her any more.

The front door opens, and Vivien and Ruth enter with shopping

Vivien That taxi just about saved my life.
Ruth Mine, too—I was ready to collapse.
Vivien I'm glad I didn't fall for that silk jersey. Not my colour.
Ruth Pink suits you.
Vivien Not that sort of pink.

Vivien and Ruth exit to the bedroom

Eric What are they going to do now? Go to bed together?
Vivien (*off*) Put the kettle on, Norman.
Eric (*to Norman*) Stay where you are. That's my kitchen.

Vivien enters

Vivien What's the matter with you? Can't I even have a cuppa when I
come home?
Eric It's not the tea I'm objecting to. It's the thought of having to drink
it in unison.
Vivien What's wrong with that?
Eric Togetherness has lost its charm.
Vivien So have you.
Eric I want some peace. Is that a crime?
Norman Ruth. Come out of there.
Vivien Honestly. Eric.

Ruth enters

Ruth Is anything the matter?
Eric Yes. I think you went into the wrong bedroom by mistake. Yours is
one floor up.
Ruth Are we in the way?
Vivien Not as far as I'm concerned.
Ruth I'll get my stuff.

Ruth exits to the bedroom

Eric Do that.
Vivien How can you be so objectionable?
Eric Years of practice.

Ruth comes back with her parcels

Norman Shall I take something?

Ruth (*giving him some parcels*) Please. (*To Vivien*) Don't forget what I said. Think it over. (*To Eric*) I hope your headache will soon be better.

Eric I haven't got a headache.

Ruth What's your excuse then?

Ruth and Norman exit upstairs

Vivien That was extremely rude.

Eric Wasn't it? But I let it pass.

Vivien Of you, I mean. Chucking them out.

Eric I didn't invite them in, in the first place.

Vivien I did. And I wish you'd made the bed. It looked thoroughly sordid. Full of newspapers and bits of toast.

Eric I wasn't expecting you to hold a reception in there.

Vivien We were only going to try our things on.

Eric How cosy!

Vivien You've been on your own all day.

Eric With Big Brother detailed to keep an eye on me. D'you know, he climbed through the bedroom window?

Vivien Oh, that was enterprising of him.

Eric We never used to live in each other's pockets like this. Sometimes we hardly saw the man from one week to the next.

Vivien You've always liked Norman.

Eric Well, at least he's harmless. But his wife is as yet an unknown quantity. And don't let her take you over.

Vivien Just because we went shopping together.

Eric I'm wondering what's tucked away behind that goody-goody veneer.

Vivien A perfectly straightforward goody-goody nature.

Eric I'm not so sure. Every now and then she looks at me in a way which I can only describe as speculative.

Vivien Don't flatter yourself.

Eric I hope I can recognize the old come-on when I see it.

Vivien Darling, she's happily married.

Eric Since when has that been the ultimate deterrent?

Vivien It wouldn't deter you, of course.

Eric What's that meant to imply?

Vivien Just remembering how you leapt to attention when she came down in those mini-shorts.

Eric Oh, that was the normal masculine reaction to cheese-cake.

Vivien I see.

Eric The point is, why was she wearing sunburnt legs all the way up to her arm-pits?

Vivien To show off her tan. It doesn't mean that she finds you irresistible. Do you want to see what I bought?

Eric Vivien.

Vivien What?

Eric I'm frightened.
Vivien Frightened?
Eric Don't you think we're running an awful risk?
Vivien What d'you mean?
Eric I'm afraid we might lose what we've got or spoil it somehow.
Vivien By making it legal? Don't be silly.
Eric At least listen to me.
Vivien I am listening.

Vivien exits to the bedroom

Eric (*calling after her*) So far we've stayed together because we wanted to. Isn't that worth a lot more than being chained together.
Vivien (*off*) We wouldn't be chained. There's always divorce.

Vivien comes from the bedroom with a bag, as Ruth comes downstairs with a similar one

Eric We're not married yet and you bring up divorce.
Vivien Because you talk as though a big, iron gate's going to shut with a clang behind you.
Eric That's what it feels like. I . . . Oh . . .

Ruth knocks and pops her head round

Ruth Sorry. I picked up the wrong one.
Vivien What? (*She looks into her own carrier*) Oh, thanks.
Ruth You're not going to show it to him, are you?
Vivien Yes, of course. (*She begins to put on her dress*)
Ruth Isn't that unlucky?
Vivien I'm not superstitious.
Ruth I am terribly. Are you superstitious, Eric?
Eric Yes. And my unlucky number's three.
Ruth I knew a girl who wouldn't tread on the cracks between paving stones. She developed a kind of sideways limp.
Eric I'm glad you told me that. It's something I've always wanted to know.
Ruth Want any help?
Vivien Just the zip.

Ruth zips Vivien up

Thanks. (*To Eric*) What d'you think?
Eric Very nice.
Ruth He means it's super.
Eric Up to now we've managed beautifully without an interpreter.
Vivien I wish you'd stop being so rude. I'm tired of apologizing for you.
Eric You don't have to. She loves it. Don't you, dear?
Vivien You might show some interest.
Eric That's exactly what I'm doing.

Ruth What are you going to wear?

Vivien Apart from a disgruntled expression?

Eric I shall wear what I always wear on Saturdays.

Vivien That old horror!

Eric My week-end uniform.

Vivien You can't possibly.

Eric It's this or nothing. My nothing's not bad, actually.

Vivien You can't be serious.

Eric It's a collar and tie all week. I have to give my neck a rest.

Vivien Aren't you going to make any effort at all?

Eric I shall shave.

Vivien I call that unreasonable.

Eric Then I won't shave.

Vivien We'll look marvellous, won't we. Me in—(*she describes the dress*) —and you in a dirty camel cardigan.

Eric You should have thought of that, shouldn't you? You should have ·bought a dirty camel dress.

Vivien begins to take off the dress

Ruth Norman could lend you a suit.

Eric I have one, thank you. I save it for funerals.

Vivien He's got dozens. All my things are pushed to the end of the rail. I think it's rotten of you, Eric.

Eric I'm a beast.

Vivien Everybody gets dressed up for a wedding.

Eric I'm sick of hearing what everybody does.

Vivien After all, you'd put on a decent suit if we were going out to dinner.

Eric Not if I'd already eaten it.

Vivien What did you say?

Eric Nothing, nothing, forget it.

Ruth He said "not if he'd already had the dinner".

Ruth exits and goes upstairs

Eric (*slamming the door behind her*) Bitch. I didn't mean it like that.

Vivien That's the most horrible thing I've ever heard in my life.

Eric It's the way you're taking it.

Vivien There's only one way to take it.

Eric Give me a chance to explain.

Vivien Don't bother. You've made yourself perfectly clear.

Eric Darling. It's going to be a Saturday like any other. We'll bring in the groceries and go on as before. Nothing will have changed. It's simply a formality.

Vivien Boring, in other words.

Eric What d'you want me to do? Act nervous? Look bashful. Pretend I'm carrying a blushing virgin over the threshold?

Vivien You'd like that, wouldn't you? If we could go back and start again?

Eric No, I wouldn't. Christ, I'm doing what you wanted. There was no stipulation about dress. Tell you what, we'll compromise. I'll stick a carnation in my cardigan.

Vivien You can stick it where you like. I know what I'm going to do.

Eric What?

Vivien Move out until we're married.

Eric I don't see what that will achieve. It's not worth it for the sake of a few days.

Vivien A few days? A few months.

Eric I don't understand—I thought it was fixed for next Saturday.

Vivien The date's been postponed to allow time for a proper engagement.

Eric A proper what? That's the stupidest thing I've heard. If we're not engaged now, what are we?

Vivien We're living together. Being engaged means living apart and you know how it's done.

Eric Tell me.

Vivien Well, you go to the pictures or for walks in the park. And you can make something together.

Eric Like . . . ? (*He gestures towards the bedroom*)

Vivien *No*. An object. Bookshelves or a rug. Ruth and Norman made a rug.

Eric I don't care if they wove the Bayeux tapestry. I'm not going to make a bloody rug.

Vivien It keeps your hands occupied. It's an excellent way of sublimating.

Eric Are you saying that we'd have to stop . . . ?

Vivien Yes. That's the whole point. Just a good night kiss and then retire to our respective quarters.

Eric In a state of acute frustration.

Vivien Do you good. Three months starvation should do wonders for a flagging appetite.

Eric Who's flagging?

Vivien You called me an old dinner.

Eric All I said was . . .

Vivien There's no need to repeat it. I heard what you said, and so did Ruth.

Eric Oh, Ruth. One of these days I'll screw that girl's neck.

Vivien I wondered what you were going to say then.

Eric Did you? That's typical. That's the way your mind works. I hope you realize that I'm not the only one who's going to feel deprived.

Vivien It won't bother me a bit.

Eric No? Have you forgotten who flung who over whose shoulder while her room-mate was out at the launderette.

Vivien I don't know what you're talking about.

Eric You reckoned she'd be away for another twenty-five minutes and set the pinger so we wouldn't lose track of the time.

Vivien Set the what?

Eric The cooking pinger. The same one which is in our kitchen now. But it didn't ping so there we were, in flagrante de pingo. I'll say this much for your friend, she came staggering in with a load of washing and didn't even blink. "Oh, sorry", she said. "If I'd known I'd have given them an extra rinse."

Vivien Are you accusing me of having seduced you?

Eric I'm reminding you that you used to have a healthy regard for the priorities.

Vivien I still have, but a temporary separation might benefit both of us.

Eric Temporary has a way of becoming permanent.

Vivien That'll be up to you, won't it? I was hoping you'd find time to call on me, once in a while.

Eric Why? Where will you be?

Vivien Not too far away. Just over your head.

Eric With them?

Vivien There's a spare room.

Eric How d'you know you can have it?

Vivien Ruth has offered me asylum.

Eric Asylum! You're not a stateless refugee.

Vivien I haven't got any papers, have I?

Eric You've got an obsession about papers. An absolute ruddy obsession.

Vivien I can't go on letting you take me for granted.

Eric What makes you think I do? For all you know I might be offering thanks to Heaven.

Vivien I've never heard you.

Eric All right. From now on I'll say my prayers aloud every night. "For what we are about to receive . . ."

Vivien That does it. That's all I need.

Vivien goes to the hall and exits upstairs

Eric (*following her into the hall*) What have I done now? (*He goes back into the flat and picks up the telephone*) Norman? . . . Yes it is. I believe you've got something of mine up there. Would you ask her to come down, please . . . You can't keep out of it . . . I'm sorry, no, you can't just sit on the fence and disclaim all responsibility for your wife's actions. What's that? I'll tell you what she's doing—she's fouling my nest.

Ruth and Vivien enter downstairs and go into the bedroom. They are followed by Norman

Norman. *Norman.* (*He bangs the phone down*)

Norman I'm sorry, old man.

Eric You're the one to feel sorry for. A bit rough, isn't it? Not married five minutes and your missus taking in lodgers.

Norman There's a spare room.

Eric You're not allowed to sublet.

Norman Taking a guest isn't subletting.

Eric Whose idea was it?

Norman The girls arranged it between them.

Eric Did they? Ruth didn't ask your permission by any chance?

Norman Why should she?
Eric You're the man of the house, aren't you?
Norman Half a house.
Eric Not half a man, I hope. I don't know, though . . .
Norman What do you mean by that?
Eric You seem to take everything lying down. No wonder Ruth walks all over you.
Norman I don't, and she doesn't.
Eric Are you quite happy about having Vivien billeted on you?
Norman No. Mainly because of you.
Eric Never mind about me. Think of your own position. You took on one, you didn't bargain for a brace. Underfoot in the bathroom, in the kitchen. With their eternal yakkity-yak. Where will you fit in? Round the edges?
Norman We'll have to manage.
Eric Poor old Norman. Landed with a wife whose mission in life is rescuing fallen women.
Norman Look—they've struck up this friendship.
Eric Ruth makes friends easily, doesn't she?
Norman She has that gift.
Eric Made a few in Tenerife, I suppose.
Norman A whole crowd of them.
Eric That's nice—as long as you're not always expected to take second place.
Norman I hope not.
Eric You'd better make a firm stand now. Tell her you object.
Norman I don't want to hurt anyone's feelings.
Eric Do it tactfully. Wear a smile. She'll admire you for it—I promise you.
Norman Right! Right.

Ruth and Vivien enter from the bedroom carrying clothes, and cross to the flat door

Ruth Open the door please, darling.
Eric Don't.
Norman What?
Eric Don't.
Norman Ah. Right. Fine. Ruth.
Ruth Hurry up.
Norman Listen, love, before you go any farther . . .
Ruth Can't you see we've both got our hands full?
Norman Yes. The thing is . . .
Ruth Quick before I drop the lot . . .

Norman opens the door and Ruth and Vivien exit upstairs, leaving him talking to the air

Eric You were magnificent.

Norman Ruth can be very determined.

Eric All the more reason to show her what you're made of. Though I must say I've eaten jelly babies with more backbone.

Norman Well, it's only for a few days. Until next Saturday.

Eric Oh, haven't you been informed? The fatal day's been postponed.

Norman Postponed?

Eric Until October.

Norman Three months?

Eric Yes, and during that time I'm supposed to do what you two did—or rather what you didn't do.

Norman I'm not with you.

Eric Vivien has in mind a carbon copy of your courtship. Pictures on Friday. Tea with Auntie on Saturday. Walk round the flipping park on Sunday—and if I'm a good boy I may be allowed to hold her hand—loosely.

Norman She's cutting off your bath water.

Eric I'm glad you find it amusing. Perhaps you can give me a few hints—on how to make rugs, for instance.

Norman Oh, no. Don't let her get you on that. That's hell!

Eric Why did you do it then? Why do you give in to her? You even let her drag you to a steaming jungle on your honeymoon.

Norman She had her heart set on it.

Eric Left you to suffer while she went out to play.

Norman I used to lie and listen to them down at the swimming pool—laughing.

Eric Said it was a mosquito bite . . .

Norman It was a tarantula.

Eric Yes—a great, hairy monster—know what you ought to do? Move down here with me for as long as Vivien stays up there.

Norman Oh, I couldn't do that.

Eric What's the matter? Too scared?

Norman You're asking a lot.

Eric It's for your own sake.

Ruth and Vivien come downstairs

Norman All the same—that's a bit drastic . . .

Eric It's your only hope.

Norman Wait a minute. Aren't you the one who's in trouble?

Eric Me? In trouble. I've got no ties, no cares, no in-laws. I'm laughing. I wish I was dead.

Ruth (*entering the flat*) One more lot and that should do it.

Norman Ruth.

Ruth What?

Norman Eric has something to say.

Eric I see. The buck stops here.

Norman I'll back you up.

Vivien (*entering the flat*) What are you plotting, Eric? Don't listen to him, Norman. Especially if he says it's for your own sake.

Eric Hang on a minute. This affects all of us.

Ruth Go on, then.

Eric Oh, a word from our sponsor. May I?

Ruth You have all my attention.

Eric That could be interesting. I have a theory, that the mere presence of a third party can cause friction between two people who are usually happy and contented. A mild joke is taken as a major insult, and a slight tiff becomes a full-scale row.

Norman Hear, hear.

Ruth What are you hear, hearing about? I bet you don't even know what he means.

Norman Yes, I do.

Ruth Explain it to me, then.

Norman It's perfectly simple. Supposing I were to say to you—in a moment of extreme anger and anguish—supposing I were to say to you . . .

Eric "You're a bossy, little cow."

Ruth What?

Norman Now, if somebody heard me say you were a bossy, little cow, you'd be furious—but if we were on our own you wouldn't mind a bit.

Ruth Just try it, that's all. Just try it and see whether I'd mind or not.

Eric Now I'd like to make a proposal.

Vivien That'll be a change.

Eric Or a proposition.

Vivien Yes, that sounds more like you..

Eric While we've got these problems of personal adjustment to sort out ..

Norman Too right we have!

Ruth Why don't you speak for yourself?

Norman Because you won't listen to me. But you hang on his every word.

Eric Oh, he's noticed. We'll have to be more careful, dear. Where was I?

Vivien Problems of personal adjustment to sort out.

Eric Thank you. The perfect secretary. Yes, for the time being we should call a halt to all social intercourse between us . . .

Vivien And the other sort.

Eric And confine our conversation to hallo and good-bye.

Ruth I should hate that.

Norman Better than putting our marriage in danger.

Ruth How?

Norman We're better on our own.

Ruth You didn't object before.

Norman A, I wasn't asked, and B, I didn't know it was for three months.

Ruth Who told you?

Norman You didn't.

Vivien Well, if that's how Norman feels . . .

Ruth Can't you see he's been got at? Anyway, everything's organized. We can't go back on it now.

Norman You'll have to.

Ruth Are you trying to make me look ridiculous?

Eric You see. The fear of losing face.

Ruth As if I'm not mistress in my own home.

Norman You're a wife not a mistress and there was that little matter of honour and obey.

Ruth It's time that was struck out of the service.

Norman You shouldn't make vows you don't intend to keep.

Ruth I said for better or for worse, too, but that doesn't mean that I shall put up with certain matters getting any worse.

Norman What certain matters?

Ruth Never mind.

Norman You can't drop great hints like that and then say "never mind". These two will think that I'm in some way lacking.

Eric Note—these two will think!

Ruth You were an utter wet blanket in the Canaries.

Norman I was under the weather.

Ruth Not too far under to flirt with a child of nature.

Norman She brought me a glass of iced water.

Ruth You could have asked me.

Norman I would have done if I could have prised you away from that tight knot of overdeveloped Swedes.

Ruth They were Dutchmen.

Norman Then so am I!

Vivien Please stop—please. I'll go to a hotel.

Ruth No, you won't.

Norman Look, if she wants to go to a hotel . . .

Ruth Why should she go to a hotel?

Norman I'm just saying that if she wants to . . .

Ruth She doesn't want to.

Vivien No, but if Norman's not happy . . .

Ruth Don't worry about Norman. It's all right with Norman. Isn't it?

Norman Are you asking me or telling me?

Ruth Both.

Norman How d'you mean—both? You say it's all right, isn't it? You make a statement and then question it. The point is, do I have a choice or don't I?

Ruth Of course you do, darling. You can take it or leave it.

Norman All right.

Norman exits upstairs

Vivien I can't force myself on him.

Ruth He said, "all right", didn't he? Let's finish moving your things.

Vivien Well, just for a night or two, and then I'll find somewhere else.
(*To Eric*) No use asking you to lend a hand, I suppose.

Eric Me?

Vivien I thought not.

Eric So why ask?
Vivien Just testing.

Vivien exits to the bedroom

Eric Why are people so horrid to me. I'm a lovely chap, really. No trouble to anyone. Oh, well—I shall soldier on. No matter what the world says I know I'm adorable. (*He pours himself a drink*)

Norman enters, carrying a pile of clothes, etc.

Good lord! He's actually done it. (*He raises his glass in a toast*) In this hour, history is being made. You're a brave man.
Norman I'm a worried man.
Eric Pour yourself a drop of courage.
Norman Thanks.
Eric No. Allow me. (*He makes a point of pouring a drink for Norman as a tribute to his courage*)
Norman (*sitting*) I hope I'm doing the right thing.
Eric Of course you are. You've got to bring her to heel now, otherwise you'll never have any authority. Your own children will treat you with contempt.
Norman We're not likely to have any, are we?
Eric You never know. You might bump into each other in the hall. It's not so bad, after all, being celibate.
Norman You've hardly started.
Eric It's growing on me, though. I'm beginning to like it. Think of the energy we'll save.

Norman jumps up with a sharp cry

What's bitten you this time?
Norman I've left a pile of stuff on the bed.
Eric So? She's bound to find out, isn't she? You can't expect to decamp without her noticing.

Vivien and Ruth enter from the bedroom with clothes

Vivien That should do it.
Eric They're like a double act, those two. I wonder which one's the straight man?

Vivien drops some things and retrieves them

Ruth (*picking up Norman's pants*) Here. There's this as well.
Vivien Those aren't mine.
Ruth Well, they're certainly not mine. They must be Eric's.
Vivien They're not Eric's. They must be Norman's.
Ruth They can't be. They fell out of your things.
Vivien I don't have Norman's knickers among my things.
Ruth That's why I say they can't be Norman's.

Vivien Look, I know they're not Eric's. I've been doing his washing and ironing for long enough.
Ruth I haven't done any washing for Norman yet.
Vivien What's he doing with everything? Throwing it away.
Ruth Drip drying mostly.
Vivien These have been ironed.
Ruth Not by me. Have you ever done his smalls?
Vivien No, I haven't.
Ruth Sorry. I thought as a neighbourly gesture . . .
Vivien We're not that neighbourly.
Ruth Well, it doesn't rain striped jockey shorts.
Vivien And Eric doesn't wear striped jockey shorts.
Ruth Who does?
Vivien Are you suggesting that I keep other men's knickers in my drawers?
Norman Er, those are mine, actually.
Ruth Are they? What were they doing out here?
Eric A very good question. Answer it.
Norman I must have dropped them.
Eric He's liable to drop his pants anywhere.
Ruth Who does them for you?
Norman What? Oh, the Chinese laundry.
Ruth I'm not incapable, you know.
Norman I'm sorry.
Eric I'll make sure he saves the next lot for you. Look out for a grubby bundle at the foot of the stairs.
Ruth Where?
Eric Let me explain. We're rearranging the house. It's going to be men only on the ground floor. That's me myself and your husband.
Ruth What?
Eric Stags downstairs. Hens—(*he clucks*)—upstairs.
Vivien Are you moving in with Eric?
Ruth What?
Eric That's right. I've granted him asylum.

Ruth runs upstairs

Vivien I see. Tit for tat.
Eric Or tat for tit. Depending on where you're standing.

Vivien exits upstairs

Norman prepares to follow, going to the hall

Come on, then.

Norman Yes, but I've got to get the rest of my stuff.

Norman is about to mount the stairs when a mass of clothes and things descends on him, as—

                    the CURTAIN *falls*

ACT II

SCENE 1

The same. Late the same evening

When the CURTAIN *rises, Eric is discovered lying on the sofa, an empty glass in his hand. He holds it out for Vivien to fill, but she is not there so he goes to the bar and helps himself. He then goes to the flat door, tripping over a sombrero on the floor. This he picks up and puts on the sofa. He wanders into the hall, then comes back again and lies on the sofa, putting the sombrero over his head*

Norman enters from the bedroom and wanders about restlessly

Norman Oh, I was looking for that. I've put everything else away.

Eric I could hear you—digging yourself in.

Norman All ship-shape now.

Eric Splendid.

Norman This ear's tingling. D'you think somebody's talking about me?

Eric I'm sure of it. What d'you suppose women talk about when they're on their own?

Norman They wouldn't discuss us in detail, though, would they?

Eric You bet they would. We'll be pegged out on their dissecting table, being scrutinized and analysed. Piece by piece.

Norman I don't like it. (*He goes to the hall*)

Eric Just a form of sport and recreation. I wish you'd settle down. Find a warm corner, turn round three times and curl up—there's a good chap.

Norman I'll be back in a minute.

Eric You're for ever nipping up to the hen-house, like a randy old rooster. What's the pretext this time?

Norman I want a book.

Eric You've got a book.

Norman I've read it.

Eric You can't have read it already.

Norman I already read it before. I hadn't realized.

Eric I see. You pick up an already read book so you can go back and change it.

Norman It wasn't intentional. (*He picks a book up from a chair*)

Eric Go on. Change your book. Change your mind. Make an idiot of yourself. Grovel.

Norman sits down and begins to read

I thought you'd read that.

Norman I can read it again, can't I? There's no law against reading the same book twice.

Eric No, indeed.

Norman reads and hums

D'you always do that?

Norman What?

Eric Hum while you're reading.

Norman I wasn't humming.

Eric Yes, you were. Can't you hear yourself?

Norman No (*He hums*)

Eric You're doing it now.

Norman I am not humming.

Eric You sound like the fridge on a warm night.

Norman I wish you'd leave me alone.

Eric I wish you'd stop humming.

Norman reads and hums

It's a sort of little tune at the back of your throat like this. Hmmmmm. Hmmmmm.

Norman Nobody's ever noticed it before.

Eric Perhaps they were too kind to mention it.

Norman They'd have mentioned it if they'd noticed it, but they haven't because I don't and I wasn't.

Eric Who's they?

Norman People I have read with. All sorts of people.

Eric Deaf ones. Do you by any chance read in bed?

Norman Yes. Until quite late.

Eric I look forward to that. Hmmmmmm. Hmmmmm. Into the small hours.

Norman hums

Right. That's enough. Time's up.

Norman What's the matter now?

Eric You've made your point. You've made your position clear. You can go back now.

Norman But I've only been here since tea-time.

Eric Really? It seems much longer. Anyway, I'm sure Ruth will have got the message—you've shown that you can be pushed so far and no farther.

Norman But what was the point of moving all my stuff down?

Eric To make it look convincing, of course.

Norman I'm all mixed up. I don't know whether I'm coming or going.

Eric (*going to the flat door*) You're going, old man. You're going to beat on the door and demand the restitution of your conjugal rights. (*He beats on the door and shouts*) Come out. We know you're in there. And throw my woman out while you're about it.

Norman I can't do that.

Eric (*ushering him into the hall*) You must. You don't want her around while you're doing the old Tarzan.

Ruth appears on the stairs

Ruth What was that? All that banging and shouting?
Eric It's Norman. I can't hold him. He's out of control.
Norman Ruthie!
Ruth Whatie?
Norman I'm coming back.
Ruth Like hell you are.

Ruth exits, and a door slams

Eric Very good. Full marks.
Norman (*sitting down*) Yes, well she'll have to come to me now.
Eric You can't just sit there.
Norman Watch me.
Eric Norman, it takes a very big person to say forgive me, you were wrong. You're that sort of person. Ring her up.

Vivien comes downstairs

Norman No.
Eric Leap up the fire-escape and press your nose to her window.
Norman I'm not moving. (*He reads*)
Vivien (*entering the flat*) Norman, you've got to make allowances. She's such a child.
Eric It's no use. He's in a black sulk. Nothing's going to shift him.
Vivien I'm sure Ruth's sorry.
Norman She will be.

Vivien sits down

Eric Are you staying?
Vivien Well, when Norman's simmered down he'll want to go back and I'd be in the way.
Eric How thoughtful. You're such a sweet girl. Hear that, old chap? The coast's clear.

Norman doesn't move

Eric There's a stunning view from the bedroom window.
Vivien Since when?
Eric Since we moved the dustbin.
Vivien Since I moved the dustbin.
Eric You can see the hydrangea.
Vivien I've seen it. And I'm going to sleep on the sofa.
Eric Oh.

Pause—Norman begins to hum

Vivien What's that funny noise?
Eric A sort of humming?
Vivien Yes.

Norman hurls his book down and rushes off upstairs. He returns, dials a number on the phone, slams the receiver down, exits to the bedroom, comes back and goes towards the kitchen

Norman I think I'll make some toast.
Eric Whatever turns you on.
Norman What's the bread situation?
Eric Oh, God.
Vivien There's plenty.
Norman Could you look at a piece?
Vivien No, thank you.
Eric And I don't eat breakfast at night.
Norman (*shouting*) You should. It saves a hell of a lot of time in the morning.

Norman exits to the kitchen

Eric He's driving me mad. He's not like this at the office, you know. We have never known him to raise his voice, turn a hair, bat an eyelid. You name it, Norman hasn't done it. And now? All to cock. Humming like a demented bee. Marriage.
Vivien Oh, nonsense.
Eric Sweetheart—if more people realized the side-effects.
Vivien What's on TV?
Eric Whatever was on six months ago. A second chance to see.
Vivien Might as well wait for the news, then.
Eric Might as well. When we're sitting together like this, don't you get the feeling that we've always been together and always will be, and nothing can ever change it?
Vivien No.
Eric There was a time when you'd agree with me.
Vivien There was a time when you could have told me that one and one made five and I wouldn't have questioned it.
Eric So what happened?
Vivien I got wise to you, my darling. I wonder if Jane would have me for a day or two while I look round for somewhere.
Eric You're full of plans, aren't you? I'll do this, I'll do that. What about me?
Vivien Yes, it does seem funny not to be putting you first. I've been doing it for so long. Darling likes this, darling wouldn't want that. Seems odd to be pleasing myself for once.
Eric Anyone would think you'd been utterly miserable for two years.

Vivien Actually, I've been very happy for most of the time.

Ruth comes downstairs

Eric Then why all this bitterness?
Vivien I wasn't meaning to sound bitter . . . (*She switches on the TV*)
Eric It's not nearly time yet.
Vivien It takes time to warm up.
Eric Not all that long. Less than a minute usually, like you.

Ruth enters the flat and sits down

Come in.
Ruth I don't see why I should be stuck up there on my own.
Eric Could it be something to do with the fact that that's your flat and this is mine?
Vivien You always say "mine" never "ours."
Eric Well, it's in my name.
Vivien Yes, the flat's in your name, but I'm not.
Eric You never let it rest, do you?

Norman enters, eating toast

You never let it rest.
Norman (*to Ruth*) You're not supposed to be down here. (*He turns off the TV*)
Ruth Why not? Vivien is.
Norman She lives here.
Ruth Well, you don't.
Norman I do now. Don't I, Eric? I'm living with you now, aren't I? (*He sits*)
Eric What? Oh, yes. If you like.
Ruth But that's practically—that's desertion.
Norman Desertion? You denied me access. I've got witnesses.
Ruth Oh, come on. Stop fooling about. And you've got butter on your chin!
Norman I don't care. (*He wipes the buttery toast on his face*)
Ruth Get up.
Norman No.
Ruth Eric!
Eric It's nothing to do with me.
Ruth (*to Norman*) I'll give you one more chance.
Norman And then what?
Ruth You'll be sorry.
Norman Ruth looks like her daddy when she's angry. He doesn't approve of me, you know. Oh, no, not at all. We had to get Mummy to twist his arm a bit to let us get married.
Ruth You imagine things.
Norman You ought to see him introduce me to his friends with a faint air

of apology. Norman doesn't play golf. Gofe, notice. Gofe. Like 'otel and bugger orff.

Ruth Yes, why don't you?

Norman A moment ago you were begging me to come back.

Ruth I said you could if you liked.

Norman Oh, thank you.

Ruth Come on, then.

Norman Yes, well, I'll bear it in mind.

Ruth Honestly. You're infuriating.

Ruth exits upstairs

Vivien She's going to cry, you know.

Norman She always does if she doesn't get her own way.

Vivien Well, don't leave her up there on her own.

Eric (*rising*) She won't be on her own, will she? You'll be with her. (*He holds the door open for Vivien*)

Vivien Are you chucking me out?

Eric I love the way you distort things. I'm falling in with your plans and you accuse me of chucking you out. (*To Norman*) I've got a feeling that I'm going to get very, very drunk tonight.

Norman You'll get help.

Eric Good old Norman. (*He pats Norman's cheeks and gets butter on his hands*)

Vivien Watch him. He's vile when he's hung over.

Eric Stop criticizing me, woman. You have forfeited all right to criticize me.

Vivien I see. You're on your own now, are you?

Eric Absolutely, Master of my Fate, Captain of my soul.

Vivien (*rising and looking towards the kitchen*) Well, I hate to tell you, Captain—but your galley's on fire.

Vivien exits upstairs

Eric Norman! You and your bloody toast.

Eric and Norman dash to the kitchen, as—

the CURTAIN *falls*

SCENE 2

The same. The following morning, Sunday.

When the CURTAIN *rises the stage is empty and the flat in darkness. Vivien comes downstairs in a dressing-gown and knocks on the bedroom door. Then she clears away some plates and glasses and an empty bottle, which she takes to the kitchen*

As Vivien returns, Norman enters from the bedroom and takes hold of her

Norman Hallo, darling.
Vivien No, it's me, Vivien.
Norman Oh, I thought you were Ruth, wearing that.
Vivien It was the first thing that came to hand. She's not down here then?
  (*She draws the curtains*)
Norman No. Why?
Vivien Have you seen her at all this morning?
Norman No. I just woke up.
Vivien Is Eric still sleeping.
Norman Like a baby.
Vivien Did he—did you both have a good night?
Norman Fairly. We had a skinful before we turned in.
Vivien Yes. I could tell. I think Ruth's gone.
Norman Gone where?
Vivien Your guess is as good as mine. I only just woke up myself. We were talking till God knows when.
Norman Perhaps she's nipped out for something.
Vivien On a Sunday morning?
Norman What time is it now?
Vivien Going for twelve. I wonder if she's gone home?
Norman Oh my God. Has she left a note?
Vivien I couldn't find one.
Norman Perhaps I should ring her people.
Vivien It's not certain she's gone to Guildford. You'd only alarm them.
Norman Probably wouldn't have got there yet, anyway. I'll drive down, I think. Yes.
Vivien Aren't you going to get dressed first?
Norman That's a point. (*He sets off towards his own flat*)
Vivien You're going the wrong way.
Norman Oh God, yes. Almost twelve did you say?
Vivien Must be by now. I'll make some coffee.
Norman Perhaps she's gone for a walk?
Vivien It's pouring. And why would she take her make-up?
Norman (*going into the bedroom*) Eric! Wake up. Ruth's gone. Gone. Fat lot you care. Where are my clothes? I can't see a bloody thing in here.

Protests from Eric as the light goes on

Eric (*off*) Watcher doing? You mad? It's Sunday.
Norman (*off*) I know it's Sunday—and I've got to go and look for my wife.
Eric (*off*) Why? Where is she?
Norman (*off*) If I knew that I wouldn't have to look for her, would I?
Eric (*off*) Who's knocking about in there?
Norman (*off*) Vivien.

Eric (*off*) Vivien?

Eric enters

Ah, she's come for me. I knew she wouldn't be able to keep away for long.

Vivien Has Norman told you?

Eric About Ruth? Silly little bitch. She'll be back in an hour.

Vivien How do you know?

Eric She's only making a gesture. If Norman's got any sense, he'll make one right back. I missed you, sweetheart.

Vivien There'll be some coffee soon.

Eric Great.

Vivien There's a filthy mess in this kitchen.

Eric Norman had to put the fire out.

Vivien With minestrone? Why don't you get dressed?

Eric Because I'm going back to bed. Aren't we?

Vivien No.

Eric Did you sleep well?

Vivien Yes, thank you.

Eric Liar.

Vivien You weren't there.

Eric Oh, you noticed. I can tell by your morning face what sort of night you've had.

Vivien As long as you had your eleven hours.

Eric I'll have you know that I was awake from two o'clock until well after six.

Vivien Well, you slept for most of yesterday. There is a limit, you know. You don't give yourself a chance to get tired.

Eric You're the one who doesn't give me the chance to get tired. Give us a kiss.

Vivien No.

Eric Why not? We're engaged, aren't we?

Vivien You chucked me out.

Eric Only so that we can start again from scratch. We're going to observe all the customs. Would you like the traditional ring? Three invisible diamonds in a vast setting?

Vivien I'd love one.

Eric And shall we start collecting a dinner service? Piece by piece.

Vivien For my bottom drawer?

Eric According to Ruth your bottom drawer's stuffed with men's knickers. She thinks we're ever so naughty. It fascinates her. She's never actually been in contact with sin before.

Vivien She can't help the way she was brought up.

Eric She's a bossy little cow, though. Give us a kiss.

Vivien No.

Vivien exits to the kitchen

Eric Then why have you come down looking bewitching in that what-is-it? What is it, anyway?

Vivien (*off*) It's one of Ruth's.

Eric It looks like one of those lines you send off for.

Vivien (*off*) Well, it's a honeymoon job.

Eric I reckon it's a con job. I wouldn't be surprised to find that you've drugged that girl and put her in the broom cupboard—so that Norman would dash out and leave us on our own.

Vivien enters with a tray of coffee and four cups

Vivien If that's what you think you'd better have your coffee black. It'll clear your head. (*She puts the tray on the drinks shelf*)

Eric My mind is as crystal. I see it all. It's typical of you, of course— being both crafty and oversexed. (*He tries to kiss Vivien*)

Vivien Be careful. (*She gives him his coffee*)

Norman enters

Norman Oh, sorry . . .

Eric Didn't anyone ever tell you to knock before you come out of a bedroom?

Norman You're all right, aren't you? You always land on your feet.

Vivien Do have some breakfast before you go out.

Norman No thanks. Excuse me.

Vivien exits to the kitchen

Eric You're not really going to Guildford, are you? Straight into the lion's den? Ruth might be there displaying her bruises and bringing Daddy up to boiling point.

Norman I'll have to risk that.

Eric Why? Play it cool. Go back to bed. Not in there, though. Use your own.

Norman I can't just do nothing and wait.

Eric Give her time and she'll come creeping home.

Vivien Don't listen to him, Norman. Use your own judgement. You know Ruth better than he does.

Eric I guarantee it, old chap. She'll return like a homing pigeon. Mine has. It's all swinging again.

Norman Just because it works for you.

Eric Try it.

Norman Too risky.

Eric It's a pity about you, Norman. You lose your nerve. That's where I score.

Vivien enters from the kitchen and exits to the bedroom

Eric Do what you like—but don't disturb us until about six this evening. If then.

Norman exits upstairs

(*Finishing his coffee*) I'll be with you in a minute, sweetheart. Don't start without me.

Vivien enters with a suitcase and goes to the door

There's no hurry to bring your stuff down.

Vivien I'm not bringing it down, I'm taking it out.

Eric Out?

Vivien Yes, I'm getting out altogether.

Eric But I thought . . .

Vivien You thought it was all swinging again, didn't you? As if I'd stay in this house alone with you.

Eric But, darling, what have you got to lose that . . .

Vivien Why don't you finish what you were going to say?

Eric Because you're so damned touchy lately.

Vivien I've got good reason to be.

Eric What happened to your sense of humour?

Vivien The joke's always on me. (*She starts to go upstairs*)

Eric (*trying to take the case*) Let me take that.

Vivien Don't strain yourself.

Eric Sweetheart . . .

Vivien Leave me alone.

Eric Have you seen it? It's pissing down out there. Let me talk to you while you pack.

Vivien I've got to get dressed first.

Eric I'll talk to you while you dress.

Vivien I'd rather you didn't.

Eric Why, what have you got to hide that I haven't already . . .

Vivien Oh, shut up.

Vivien exits upstairs. Eric follows. Ruth enters from the street with a case and mac which she leaves in the hall, and enters Eric's flat. Eric comes downstairs in pain

Eric You didn't learn that from me. What are you? A black belt or something? That's a wicked knee you've got there. (*He enters his own flat and meets Ruth*)

Ruth Is Norman anywhere about?

Eric He's gone to look for you.

Ruth Oh dear.

Eric You do complicate life, don't you?

Ruth I'm a mess.

Eric If you say so. Don't cry. Your eyes will run down your face.

Ruth What does it matter? You hardly look at me anyway.

Eric Could you look at a cup of coffee?

Ruth Now you're making fun of me.

Eric Believe me, at this moment, fun is the last thing I feel like making. Go on. It's fresh.

Ruth Shall I help myself? (*She pours herself coffee*)

Eric Well, you're not incapable, are you? As you declared so forcibly last night. Why on earth did you clear off without a word to anyone?

Ruth I wanted to go home. I got as far as Waterloo but then I couldn't face them. Daddy would only go purple and upset Mummy—so I took a taxi back.

Eric Mummy upsets easily, does she?

Ruth Over the least little thing.

Eric A little thing like your husband rolling up and telling them he doesn't know where you are?

Ruth So what did he have to go for?

Eric You'd have been deeply hurt if he hadn't.

Ruth I might have been impressed. You'd have sat tight, wouldn't you?

Eric You'd better telephone Daddy and warn him. Tell him that Norman's on his way.

Ruth I'd have to say we'd had a row.

Eric Well, you can't very well say he's popping over to borrow the lawn-mower.

Ruth I've never seen you in pyjamas before.

Eric No?

Ruth They're a nice colour.

Eric Marks and Sparks.

Ruth Where's Vivien?

Eric She's upstairs. Packing.

Ruth Is she moving down here again?

Eric No, she's moving out—any minute now.

Ruth Oh.

Eric Get on with it. Norman's probably doing ninety and there won't be much traffic about.

Ruth There's a button off.

Eric You make your phone call. (*He gets a dressing-gown from the bedroom*) What are you waiting for?

Ruth You. You haven't told me what to say yet.

Eric This is the first time I've ever known you stuck for words.

Ruth Don't be beastly. And why have you put your dressing-gown on?

Eric I felt a draught somewhere.

Ruth It's warm.

Eric Make your call.

Ruth You don't want to know, do you?

Eric What's the number?

Ruth I'll do it myself. (*She dials*)

Eric Any luck?

Ruth There's no answer.

Eric Wait. Perhaps they're not up yet. (*He takes the receiver*)

Ruth No. No answer.

Eric (*listening*) Not surprising, really. "At the third stroke it will be twelve-fourteen precisely."

Ruth You must think I'm awful.

Eric (*putting the receiver down*) I haven't made up my mind yet, but I am wondering how, in the short time you've been under this roof, you've managed to dislocate the entire household.

Ruth And who was it thought of stags down here, hens upstairs?

Eric I didn't begin the general reshuffle.

Ruth Indirectly you did, by upsetting Vivien.

Eric It wouldn't have occurred to her to be upset, if you hadn't suggested it to her. Whenever I looked round, there was Ruthie, stirring away with her little wooden spoon.

Ruth I didn't mean any harm.

Eric Then God knows what havoc you'd cause if you really tried.

Ruth begins to cry

Oh, come on. Cheer up. (*He puts his arm round her*) Nothing's beyond repair. Get a grip on yourself.

Ruth flings her arms round him

Not on me—what the . . .

As Eric struggles to free himself Vivien comes downstairs and leaves. Eric tries to run after her, then returns

Ruth Has she gone?

Eric Yes. I might have stopped her if you hadn't been wound round my neck like a bloody python.

Ruth Why don't you run after her?

Eric That shows how little you know me. Although if I'd been dressed— I didn't think she'd go. Not really.

Ruth You can't blame her for wanting to start again on a proper footing.

Eric We were like that. Interlocked. Interdependent. If that's not a proper footing, what is?

Ruth Some people would call it irregular.

Eric D'you realize you almost got yourself clobbered then? You'd better go. Something about you irritates me to the point where I might forget my lifelong code of non-violence.

Ruth I like you when you're angry.

Eric Go and infuriate Norman then. You shouldn't find it difficult.

Ruth Norman's very placid.

Eric Keep trying. I've got complete faith in your ability.

Ruth Aren't you horrible?

Eric I do my best to please. Why don't you go and spruce the place up for when your husband comes home? Scatter a few cushions. Make it look like a love-nest.

Ruth He won't be home for ages yet.

Eric Then you'll have plenty of time, won't you? Surprise him. Knock up a batch of rock-buns.

Ruth I thought I was to infuriate him.

Eric I should think you've already done that. Sent him scouring the Home Counties on a day like this.

Ruth Can't I wait down here?

Eric If you promise to behave yourself. (*He takes some newspapers from the bookshelf*) Which do you want? The highbrow stuff or the indecent assaults.

Ruth I don't feel like reading, thanks.

Eric Mind if I catch up on the week's news? Events at home have tended to crowd the world out.

Ruth Norman admires you tremendously.

Eric I'm so glad. I'm crazy about him, too.

Ruth He says that women have beaten a path to your door.

Eric That was the man who built a better mousetrap.

Ruth He says that you're probably unrivalled in the field.

Eric In the where? Oh, I see. Well, I shall know where to apply if I ever want a reference.

Ruth (*undoing her blouse*) Look, what I'm trying to tell you is that he wouldn't mind, even if he found out, but he wouldn't find out because we wouldn't tell him. (*She takes off her blouse*)

Eric What are you going?

Ruth My tan's beginning to fade.

Eric Don't move. Don't undo another thing.

Ruth You're not going to let me down, are you?

Eric I wasn't aware that I'd promised you anything.

Ruth You might co-operate a bit. It's not very easy for me.

Eric Stop doing it then.

Ruth But I've got to know and who else can I approach? At least we wouldn't get involved and it would only be this once and then I'd know.

Eric Know what? What is it you want to know?

Ruth Whether it's always no good, or whether it's just no good with Norman.

Eric Give it a chance. You've still got your L-plates up. You can't expect instant rapture.

Ruth But that's the whole trouble. I don't know what to expect, do I? I've got nothing to compare it with.

Eric Is that what you want me for? A British Standard Measure?

Ruth You ought to put back into the world something of what you've taken out. Like passing on craftsmanship.

Eric We're not making violins.

Ruth All the same, you have a duty towards women.

Eric Norman has lumbered himself with a genuine original here. No wonder the poor chap's out of his depth.

Ruth He'll benefit too, indirectly.

Eric I hope he'll appreciate that. What would I say? Here's your wife back. I've been running her in for you.

Ruth You won't have to say anything because he won't know.

Eric I am shocked.

Ruth Shocked? You?

Eric Shaken rigid and shocked beyond belief. What would Daddy think?

Ruth I don't care. It's his rotten fault I'm as green as grass.

Eric Besides, I'm a married man.

Ruth You're what?

Eric Well, practically—to all intents and purposes.

Ruth Married is exactly what you're not. What's more, married is exactly what you don't want to be.

Eric All the same, I consider myself bound.

Ruth Bound to what?

Eric You're a persistent little bitch, aren't you?

Ruth You're a bachelor, Eric. A free lance. There's nothing to stop you. I think you're terrified.

Eric Who wouldn't be?

Ruth I mean you're afraid of falling short of your reputation.

Eric I hope you don't imagine that I swallowed all that stuff about beating paths through the fields and so on. The most Norman might have said was, "Eric does all right."

Ruth Ah, but it was the way he said it.

Eric Aroused your curiosity?

Ruth Aroused my interest. What about you? How's your interest?

Eric I see there's trouble in the Middle East again.

Ruth You're just not trying.

Eric What makes you think I'm all that keen?

Ruth You mean you don't want to?

Eric There's always that possibility.

Ruth I'm unattractive in other words.

Eric I didn't say you were unattractive. Nobody could say that. In fact, you're absolutely—not bad.

Ruth starts to cry

Eric There's a box of Kleenex behind the aspidistras.

Ruth No, there isn't.

Eric There should be. You can't rely on anything these days.

Ruth No, you can't.

Eric If you want me to make love to you, stop grizzling. Nothing is less inviting than a grizzler.

Ruth I've stopped now.

Eric Good for you. How did you get that colour? Use a lot of oil, did you?

Ruth Ambre Solaire.

Eric Ambre Solaire.

Ruth You rub it in.

Eric Mmmmm.

Ruth Eric . . .

Eric kisses her

Eric Good lord! Hot chocolate sauce!

Ruth starts for the bedroom

Hey, where are you going? Come back.

Ruth exits to the bedroom

If you think you can inveigle me into doing something we'll both regret
. . . Norman's my friend! Norman's my friend. Norman's my friend. I'd
be an absolute bastard! Who says I'm not?

Eric exits to the bedroom

*Norman enters from the street, sees Ruth's things in the hall and goes
upstairs*

The telephone rings

Eric dashes in, followed by Ruth

Let me answer it. It might be Vivien.
Ruth Or Norman.
Eric You're right. It is. Hallo, Norman.
Ruth Don't tell him I'm here.
Eric I'm sorry. I missed that. There's crackling on the line—a bit of
crackling . . . Who? Ruth? No, I thought she'd gone home. Where are
you, anyway? . . . I know you're on the phone, but where's the phone? . . .
Oh. (*Norman has rung off and Eric replaces the receiver*) I shall go to hell
for this. He's in Woking.
Ruth What's he going to do?
Eric (*reaching for a book*) Might go on to Guildford or might come
straight back. What time is it now?
Ruth There's no time to read.
Eric I want to look something up.
Ruth Don't tell me you're rusty.
Eric It's an R.A.C. handbook, not the *Khama Sutra*. I'm trying to work
out how long we've got.
Ruth I say, you don't take any chances, do you?
Eric You're not dealing with am amateur, you know. Hmmmm. Woking.
Pass me that pencil. (*He mutters calculations*) Sorry to keep you hanging
about—but time spent in preliminary research has saved many a dodgy
situation. Yes. (*He puts the book down*) Let's hope he gets stuck behind
a lorry. Trouble is, I usually fall asleep.
Ruth I never do.
Eric You might this time.
Ruth Oh, I hadn't thought of that.

Eric You've got to think of everything. Secret of my success.
Ruth I know—alarm clock! We've got two. Wedding presents. One's in a leather case. (*She starts to go upstairs*)
Eric (*calling her back*) No, don't bother. We can use the pinger.
Ruth (*returning*) The what?
Eric The cooking pinger.
Ruth Oh, of course. I remember seeing it.

Ruth exits to the kitchen for the pinger

Eric Off she goes to get it. Splendid. I do like a girl with initiative.

Ruth enters, singing away

Ruth It's quite loud, isn't it?
Eric Give it to me. You have to set it properly or it doesn't go off and that could be disastrous.
Ruth Ruins the Yorkshire pud.
Eric Yes. What a versatile piece of equipment. I bet the manufacturers would be astonished at the variety of its uses. There.

Ruth goes to the bedroom

Eric Hey, wait for me.

Eric exits to the bedroom.

Vivien enters from the street and crosses to the bedroom door

Vivien Eric? Eric?
Eric (*off*) Is that you, Vivien?
Vivien Of course it is. Who else has got a key to this flat? (*She tries the door and finds it locked*) Aren't you going to let me in?
Eric (*off*) No.
Vivien Why? It's only me.
Eric (*off*) Yes, exactly.
Vivien Eric!

Eric enters in a dressing-gown

Eric Here I am.
Vivien Why did you lock the bedroom door?
Eric Safety first. Security reasons.
Vivien We've got nothing anyone would want.
Eric That's what you think.
Vivien Go on then. I'm waiting.
Eric What for?
Vivien For you to look smug and say you were expecting me.
Eric I wasn't expecting you. Definitely not. You can quite safely say that I was not expecting you.

Vivien Darling, for once you're not going to crow over me. You could if you wanted to.

Eric I don't want to crow. No. No crow. (*He hides Ruth's blouse in the drinks cupboard*)

Vivien I didn't get very far, did I? Sat in Lyons with a cup of tea I couldn't drink—and I thought, what am I doing here? And . . . You're not listening, are you?

Eric What?

Vivien I was telling you what I did.

Eric When?

Vivien While I was out.

Eric You came back.

Vivien Yes, looks as if I did.

They kiss and start for the bedroom

Eric No, darling. We mustn't go in there.

Vivien Why not?

Eric There's a—there's a bed in there.

Vivien No.

Eric And you know what that can lead to.

Vivien So who's complaining?

Eric Aren't you forgetting something?

Vivien I haven't forgotten a thing.

Eric What about the new rules? Three months of nothing but rugs and bookshelves. Sublimating like beavers.

Vivien Oh, that.

Eric Yes, that. You'll be sorry if you weaken. It's like giving up smoking. If you can last out the first couple of days, you've got it beaten.

Vivien Who wants to beat it?

Eric We do. We want to start again on a proper footing.

Vivien Have you got somebody in there?

Eric Whatever gave you that idea?

Vivien Because that's exactly what you would do. Bring up the reserves.

Eric Use your head, darling. Have I had time to rustle somebody up, bring them up, butter them up and get them into bed—I mean, even I, unrivalled in the field . . .

Vivien So why are you behaving like this?

Eric Like what?

Vivien Like you're making damned sure I don't get into the bedroom.

Eric Why don't we have a drink?

Vivien Why not? After all, there's no hurry.

Eric Scotch and water.

Vivien O.K. Where's the scotch? (*She goes towards the drinks cupboard*)

Eric In the . . . (*He remembers that Ruth's blouse is hidden in the drinks cupboard*) No, no, I'll get it. Leave it to me. You sit down and relax.

Vivien moves away from the drinks cupboard, even more surprised and suspicious. Then banging is heard from the bedroom

Vivien You have got somebody in there. Don't worry. I'm not going in. I'll wait for her to come out.

Eric We didn't do anything.

Vivien You were going to.

Eric Well, that's not the same.

Vivien The thought is as bad as the act.

Eric No, it isn't. It isn't as good, either. (*He laughs*) Sorry.

Vivien As long as you don't expect me to laugh.

Eric Put yourself in our position. We were both feeling pretty miserable.

Vivien So was I. But I didn't throw myself under the first man I saw.

Eric It wasn't like that.

Vivien Who is she?

Eric You're going to find this hard to believe.

Vivien Is it somebody I know?

Eric Yes—but the most unlikely person.

Vivien They're all likely with you around.

Eric You'll be amazed.

Vivien Try me.

Eric Come on out!

Norman enters from the bedroom

Vivien stares at him, horrified

Vivien Oh, my God.

Eric No!

Vivien Oh, Eric. You were right—it's the last person I'd have dreamed of.

Norman How d'you suppose I feel about it?

Vivien Well, I imagine you consented.

Norman Did I hell! I'm going to kill him.

Vivien No, don't. Violence never solved anything. He needs help.

Norman What about me?

Vivien You as well. I'm trying to understand.

Norman Believe me, you wouldn't find it difficult if you'd known him as long as I have.

Vivien What?

Eric Just a minute, just a minute. Norman. She thinks it's us. Us.

Norman How d'you mean? Us?

Eric You and me.

Norman You and me?

Eric Me and you then. She's got the idea we've been taken a little queer. Oh God, you're so bloody thick.

Norman *What?*

Eric The penny's dropped. It's because she saw you coming out of there, where you had no business to be.

Norman I live here now, remember. I'm the other stag.

Eric How's Woking?

Norman I don't know, I haven't been there.

Eric Cunning bastard.
Norman It takes a thief to catch a thief.
Vivien What are you two talking about? What's been going on?
Eric Something's rather more normal than you've been imagining.
Vivien It was a girl, then. Where is she?
Norman There was no she.
Eric No she?
Norman No. Go and look if you like.
Vivien All right. I will.

Vivien goes to the bedroom. There is silence

Eric (*to Norman*) How?
Norman What climbs down can also climb up.
Eric You're a pal.
Norman I'll kill you later.

Vivien returns

Eric Satisfied?
Vivien Mmmmm. I thought you'd gone to look for Ruth?
Norman I found Ruth.
Vivien Did you? Where?
Eric What Norman means is that he tracked her down, and she's on her way home now. Wouldn't you say so, old man? On her way home?
Norman Very likely.
Vivien But where did . . .
Eric Hold on. It's your turn now. What's your explanation? You shoot out of the house and go and lurk in Lyons with a cup of tea you can't drink. I'd adjusted myself to the prospect of celibacy—in fact, I was beginning to enjoy it—wasn't I, Norman? And then you reappear taking up an entirely different position from the one you were holding when you left—and accuse my friend and I of being a pair of pouffes.
Vivien I beg your pardon.
Eric Granted.
Vivien And yours.
Norman That's all right. Anybody can make a mistake.
Eric I'm glad you take that view, Norman. Now I'll go and get dressed—with your permission.
Vivien Carry on.
Eric Thank you.

Eric exits to the bedroom

Vivien Something doesn't add up. He as good as admitted . . .
Norman (*trying to leave*) Well, if you'll excuse me . . .
Vivien No, you don't. I want to talk to you.
Norman I have to see Ruth.

Vivien I thought she wasn't home yet.

Norman She isn't, but I'd like to get everything straightened out. Up.

Vivien Are you covering up for Eric?

Norman Eric can do his own covering up. He's an expert. And I'd like to offer you a word of advice.

Vivien Oh?

Norman Leave him. He's no damned good, never has been and never will be.

Vivien That's a nice way for a friend to talk.

Norman It's a waste of time being loyal to Eric.

Vivien You only resent him because Ruth sort of—you know.

Norman You know sort of what?

Vivien She thinks he's dishy, doesn't she? She makes that pretty obvious. Whenever he looks at her she wriggles.

Ruth enters from the stairs

Norman He shouldn't look at her then.

Vivien He can't help it. It's the natural masculine reaction to cheese-cake.

Norman Don't call my wife cheese-cake.

Vivien Oh, go away, Norman. We'd better stick to just hallo and good-by. We're all getting in each other's hair.

Ruth appears in the hall, Norman dashes out to intercept her

Norman Where d'you think you're going?

Ruth Home.

Norman You've just come from there. Look who's here.

Ruth Stop it. You're hurting me. Hallo, Vivien.

Vivien Hallo. You back already?

Ruth Yes. (*To Norman*) Let go of me.

Vivien What did they say?

Ruth Who?

Vivien Your people, of course.

Ruth They said—they said my place was with my husband, no matter what.

Vivien Hardly worth going to hear that.

Ruth It made a change.

Norman Some people like a change.

Ruth Some people need a change. Anyway, you came back jolly smartly yourself, didn't you?

Vivien How did you know I'd gone?

Ruth (*hesitating*) I had a feeling you would.

Vivien Intuition.

Ruth Yes.

Vivien Remarkable.

Ruth Where's Eric?

Norman Never mind. Where's Eric? I'm here.

Ruth Yippee.

Vivien He's getting dressed.
Ruth My goodness. Doesn't he get up late.

Eric enters from the bedroom

Eric Ah, Ruth's down. Home. Everybody's come home.
Vivien Except you.
Eric I'm here, aren't I?
Vivien But you didn't go anywhere.
Eric Somebody's got to stay behind and hold the baby—keep the home fires burning—as it were.
Vivien Why are you all slicked up like that?
Eric This is in your honour, my darling. I'm taking you out to lunch.
Vivien Oh, that's nice. Why?
Eric You're so suspicious. I go to all this trouble and all you can say is Why.
Vivien It's just that I know you so well.
Eric Then you should know that I don't put on a dark suit for nothing.
Vivien That's true.
Eric Gold links, silk tie, winning smile. You're a lucky girl, d'you know that?
Vivien I should count my blessings.
Eric You should make a list.
Vivien Oh, Eric!

Eric and Vivien kiss

Norman Come on, Ruth. I want to talk to you.
Eric Yes. Run along, dear. Don't leave anything behind.
Ruth I haven't.
Eric That then, would appear to be that.
Norman For the moment, yes.
Eric It's all water under the bridge.
Norman Mucky water.

The pinger goes off. Ruth puts a hand over her mouth guiltily

Eric My egg's cooked.

Eric exits to the kitchen, Vivien to the bedroom. Both return immediately Eric with an egg in a cup on a plate, Vivien with the pinger

Vivien Since when have you taken to boiling eggs in the bedroom? (*She puts the pinger on the drinks shelf*)
Eric Late breakfast again. Oh, I've forgotten the salt.
Vivien (*grabbing the egg*) It's raw. I've a good mind to make you eat it. On second thoughts, have you ever tried an egg face pack, Ruth? It does wonders for a fading tan.
Eric Vivien. Control yourself.
Vivien Why should I? Nobody else does.

Norman (*taking the egg*) Here. Now Ruth. Yerch. (*It cracks in his hand*)

Ruth tries to mop him up with a Kleenex from the shelf. He is clumsy and she gets egg on herself. She kicks him, and throws the Kleenex at Vivien

Eric Let's try to behave like civilized people.

Vivien Civilized people have been known to behave like beasts.

Eric Only under stress.

Vivien I am under stress.

Eric So was I.

Vivien Don't give me that. One night without me and you make a grab for the lodger's lady.

Norman I own my half of the house.

Vivien You knew, didn't you?

Norman I walked in on them.

Eric Window climbing again. May I point out that the fire-escape is only to be used in an emergency.

Norman This was an emergency.

Ruth Eric's right. It shouldn't be used for invading people's privacy.

Norman Or for making a quick get-away.

Ruth Don't worry. I'm not going to make a habit of it.

Vivien A habit of what? Getting laid or being rumbled?

Norman Why, though? For god's sake, you're not a nymphomaniac, are you?

Ruth No, I'm not.

Norman Well, are you in love with him or something?

Ruth No. I don't expect you to understand, but it was purely in the spirit of scientific research.

Vivien Well, of course.

Eric It wasn't Ruth's fault. I talked her into it.

Norman You must be a super salesman.

Vivien He is but the customer's still got to be willing. I'll get myself ready for that lunch—if it's still on.

Vivien goes into the bedroom

Eric Sure, unless you'd prefer an omelette.

Eric goes to the kitchen

Ruth What are you looking so miserable for?

Norman Sorry. Next time I find you in bed with a bloke and a cooking pinger I'll laugh like a hyena.

Ruth I never will again. It was only an experiment.

Norman Don't go on about it.

Ruth Oh, darling. You shouldn't have found out.

Norman Is that supposed to make it better.

Ruth I was so glad to see you.

Norman You didn't look overjoyed.

Ruth I was, though. I'd got myself into awfully deep water. You'll have to look after me, Norman.

Norman puts his arm round her

Eric looks out from the kitchen and goes back. Norman and Ruth go to the hall, and upstairs

(*As they exit*) I didn't sleep very well last night. Did you?
Norman No. Eric kicks.
Ruth So does Vivien.
Norman Self-defence, I expect.
Ruth They're a funny couple.
Norman Yes.
Ruth Not like us.
Norman No.
Ruth We're all right, aren't we?
Norman We're going to be.

Ruth and Norman go into their flat

Vivien enters from the bedroom, Eric from the kitchen

Vivien You ready?
Eric Is all forgiven?
Vivien No, I'm just hungry. Look at that.

It starts to rain

Eric Know what I read in the *Observer*?
Vivien Don't tell me you've had time to look at the papers as well?
Eric I try to lead a full life. Apparently, this has been the worst July for seventy-three years.
Vivien I can well believe it. (*In putting the sherry bottle away she finds Ruth's blouse, and drops it on to his lap*)
Eric When I'm married . . .
Vivien What did you say?
Eric I said, when I'm married, I shall feel a damn sight safer.
Vivien You don't have to, you know.
Eric I know I don't have to, but after two years I reckon a chap's entitled to some . . .
Vivien Status?
Eric That's the word.
Vivien What about that lunch then?
Eric There's plenty of time. They're open until three.

Eric opens the bedroom door gallantly for Vivien. She exits to the bedroom. He follows her, then returns for the pinger. As Eric goes back into the bedroom—

the CURTAIN *falls*

FURNITURE AND PROPERTY LIST

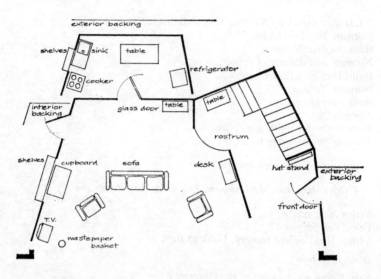

ACT I

SCENE 1

On stage: IN SITTING-ROOM:

TV set. *On it: Radio Times*

Bookshelves. *On upper shelves:* books including R.A.C. Handbook.
On bottom shelf: drinks, including sherry and assorted glasses.
In cupboard below: assorted bottles and glasses

Occasional table. *On it:* vase

Desk. *On it:* writing materials, pencil, telephone, lamp

Sofa and cushions

2 armchairs

On floor by TV set: waste-paper basket

Carpet

Window curtains

IN KITCHEN:

Cooker (partially hidden and non-practical)

Sink and taps (non-practical). *Under it:* cloths

Refrigerator

Table. *On it:* remains of breakfast for two

Shelves. *On them:* bowl of oranges, time-clock pinger, dressing

IN HALL:
Hat-stand
Stair carpet

Off stage: Wet umbrella, bags of assorted shopping, bunch of flowers (Vivien)
Briefcase (Eric)
4 suitcases (Norman)
Glass of milk (Ruth)

SCENE 2

Strike: Dirty glasses
Briefcase, mac

Off stage: Shopping bag and parcels, including dress (Vivien)
Shopping bag and parcels (Ruth)
Pile of clothes, including pair of men's pants (Vivien and Ruth)
Pile of clothes (Norman)

ACT II

SCENE 1

Set: Empty glass by sofa
Sombrero on floor

Off stage: Slice of toast and butter (Norman)

SCENE 2

Strike: Sombrero

Set: Curtains closed
Plates, glasses and empty bottle about on floor
Newspapers on drinks shelf
Box of Kleenex on drinks shelf
Raw egg in cup on plate in kitchen

Off stage: Tray of coffee for four, with coffee-pot, sugar, cream, cups, saucers,
spoons
Suitcase (Vivien)
Suitcase (Ruth)

LIGHTING PLOT

Practical fittings required: pendant, wall-brackets, desk lamp
    Interior. A flat. The same scene throughout

ACT I, Scene 1. Evening

To open: Effect of late summer afternoon, rain outside
No cues

ACT I, Scene 2. Afternoon

To open: Effect of afternoon light
No cues

ACT II, Scene 1. Late evening

To open: All interior lights on. Blue exterior
No cues

ACT II, Scene 2. Morning

To open: Daylight outside, but curtains drawn and interior dim

Cue 1	**Vivien** opens curtains	(Page 33)
	Bring up lighting to full daylight except off in bedroom	
Cue 2	**Norman** exits to bedroom	(Page 33)
	Snap on offstage bedroom light	
Cue 3	**Ruth** and **Norman** exit	(Page 49)
	Dim general lighting slightly	

EFFECTS PLOT

ACT I

SCENE 1

Cue 1 As CURTAIN rises   (Page 1)
     Effect of rain

SCENE 2

Cue 2 As CURTAIN rises   (Page 12)
     Telephone rings

ACT II

SCENE 1

No cues

SCENE 2

Cue 3 **Norman** goes upstairs   (Page 41)
     Telephone rings
Cue 4 **Norman:** "Mucky water."   (Page 47)
     Pinger rings
Cue 5 **Eric:** "Is all forgiven?"   (Page 49)
     Build up rain effect